The Universal Parish Priest

by
Josephine Robinson

All booklets are published thanks to the generous support of the members of the Catholic Truth Society

CATHOLIC TRUTH SOCIETY
PUBLISHERS TO THE HOLY SEE

Contents

EARLY LIFE

Childhood

Pope John XXIII was baptised Angelo Giuseppe on the day of his birth, 25 November 1881. His parents were Giovanni Battista and Marianna Roncalli. They lived, as part of an extended family, in the village of Sotto il Monte, Bergamo in Northern Italy.

Sotto il Monte, literally, 'under the mountain', remained for the Pope a picture of home, a special place, a little world of family warmth and of deep piety. There was, however, nothing of the fairy tale about it: they worked hard and sometimes differences and resentments occurred. The household consisted not only of Giovanni and Marianna and their children, of whom Angelo was the fourth of ten, but also a closely related family with ten children. The head of them all was an unmarried brother of Giovanni's grandfather, called Zaverio, known as *'barba'* (the beard), who was well read and intelligent and had a deep faith. He was also concerned with the difficulties of life for poor people. He it was who took the baby Angelo to be baptised and stood as godfather. The ceremony took place; there was no other celebration.

The Roncallis were tenant farmers who paid their rent by means of half their produce, and this inevitably left them insecure, because of the vagaries of weather and markets. Writing his spiritual testament in 1954, when he was Patriarch of Venice, he described his family as 'respected' and 'beloved'. He also wrote that they ate polenta, rather than bread and that clothes and also shoes, which were worn for church, had to last; 'and yet, when a beggar appeared at the door of our kitchen, when the children - twenty of them - were waiting for their bowl of vegetable soup, there was always room for him and my mother would hasten to seat this stranger alongside us.'

Their work was hard, though it was varied by the demands of each season. They toiled as their family had toiled for many generations. Their pleasures lay in the year of the Church with its feasts, prepared for by fasts, and by different devotions, lovingly followed. Hebblethwaite, in his biography quotes Pope John's reminiscence of being taken, by his mother with the other children, on pilgrimage to a shrine of Our Lady, a kilometre out of the village. Of the five small children, (Angelo was four years old) two had to be carried and another baby was on the way, so that their progress was slow and when they arrived the chapel was full and they could not get in. Marianna lifted up Angelino, as he was called as a child, to look through the window and said 'Look how beautiful the Madonna is! I have consecrated you wholly to her.' 'This' Pope John recalled 'is the first clear memory I have of my childhood.' Members of the family, like many country people, were not demonstrative with their feelings, but Pope John spoke of his mother with deep affection, saying how 'lucid' her conscience was and how she was loved and venerated by her family and beyond. He described his father in his *Journal*, writing while he was in the seminary in Rome, as 'simple and good' and himself, by contrast, as 'full of malice'.

He wrote in a letter to his brother about 'all the brides who have come to rejoice the Roncalli family, and those who have left us to increase the happiness of new families, of different names, but of similar ways of thinking. Oh the children, the children; what a wealth of children and what a blessing!'.

When, as Pope, he was first carried on the *Sedia Gestatoria*, on the shoulders of the bearers, he said, *sotto voce* 'It's windy up here' and then he remembered being carried on his father's shoulders, as a child, when he was too small to be able to see a religious procession. He wrote in a letter, 'The secret of everything is to let oneself be carried by God, and so to carry Him to others'. Very early in life, he knew he wanted to be a priest. He was allowed to make his First Holy Communion, in the village church, at the age of seven, which was very unusual at that time.

Ernesto Balducci in his book on Pope John XXIII describes how the 'fundamental quality of his holiness lies in his fidelity to childhood, seen as harmony between the "kingdom of heaven" and the kingdom of this world.' He recognised no tension between 'nature' and 'grace'.

He started his education at the village school, and when he was nearly nine he was sent as a day-boy to the Episcopal college at Celana, some way from Sotto il Monte. The Latin master was fierce and 'made me forget what little I knew. It was a disaster.'

At this point, the holy and kindly parish priest of Sotto il Monte offered to tutor Angelino to prepare him for entry into the junior seminary at Bergamo. Angelino's intelligence and taste for study were awakened and he already longed to be a priest. Although his education enabled him to receive academic degrees and attain a level of learning far beyond that of his family, he did not turn his back on them, and was always aware that parents are the first educators of their children. The letter that the then Bishop Roncalli wrote to his parents from Bulgaria in 1930, when he was nearly fifty, is often quoted. He says that despite all he had learned from books and lectures, 'what I learned from you remains the most precious and important ...' That letter must have brought both joy and re-assurance to them. The truth of it is clear. They taught him that God's love is pre-eminent and demands a living response. Throughout his life, whether as priest, bishop, nuncio or Pope, he retained a simplicity in his spiritual life, which stretches back to his family and the immediacy of their faith. It became a gift to the whole Church.

The seminarian

Angelo entered the seminary when he was nearly twelve years old, knowing that this was the preparation for the life he believed the Lord wanted him to live and which he longed for. He entered fully into the life of the seminary and from the age of fourteen he kept a spiritual diary as a guide to his progress (or regress) in the spiritual life.

His *Journal of a Soul* follows his spiritual life through to old age. After some hesitation, he gave permission for it to be published after his death. The early entries were written on lined notebooks and shortly before his death, his secretary showed them to him again. Mgr. Loris Capovilla reported later that his eyes filled with tears when he re-read, after so many years, the first entries and he said 'I was a good boy, innocent, somewhat timid. I wanted to love God at all costs and my one idea was to become a priest, in the service of simple souls who needed patient and attentive care. Meanwhile, I had to fight an enemy within me, self-love...I was troubled about my distractions during prayer...I took everything very seriously and my examinations of conscience were detailed and severe...Now, at a distance of more than sixty years, I

can look upon these first spiritual writings of mine as if
they had been written by someone else...'. As it
happened, Don Angelo Roncalli never had the parish he
longed for and was never at the day to day service of the
simple souls he hoped to care for. 'Don' was the usual
title of a priest in Italy at the time. His first 'parish' was
the Province of the Three Venetias, when he became
Patriarch and he loved his work as pastor as much as he
had expected to. As a seminarian, for all his longing for
the care of 'simple souls', he enjoyed doing well in his
studies and often rebuked himself in his *Journal* for
showing off.

The seminary itself was run on austere and rigorous
lines in order to prepare the young men for the gift that is
priesthood. Every priest was to have this gift imprinted
on him so that no-one he met could be unaware of the
great graces that he had received and the responsibilities
that he carried. Later in life, Pope John XXIII remarked
that the house was cold and the food was bad, but the
seminary was where he wanted to be. He made for
himself a little rule of life, to supplement even the
rigorous one, given to priests and seminarians from the
great sixteenth century Council of Trent. Trent urges
them, among fidelity to prayer and repentance, to
maintain the 'custody of the eyes', keeping eyes to the
floor, in order to avoid looking around. They are to

behave constantly in a manner which is 'grave, controlled and full of religious feeling.' Angelo concurred in this.

In the 1880's, these rules were examples of the Church's continuing defence of herself against 'the world' and, in Italy in particular, against a secularist nation, which had in living memory, expelled the Pope from the Papal States. The loss was still raw and the Pope as 'the Prisoner of the Vatican' the result of it. It took years before Pius XII stated his understanding that the loss of temporal power was in fact a blessing for the Church. No-one, thereafter could confuse the Pope with any earthly ruler. The tiny Vatican State emphasised the Church's universal, spiritual role.

Angelo's private little rule began with the importance of choosing a good spiritual director. On getting up, he wrote, he should offer private prayer (lasting fifteen minutes, he suggested); he should hear '(or better serve)' Mass. Fifteen minutes of spiritual reading had to be fitted in and at night an examination of conscience. A visit to the Blessed Sacrament was included and various prayers were to be recited. Daily communion was not yet permitted - Pius X inaugurated it in 1903. Every week, he was to go to Confession and he did this all his life. When he was Pope, he chose to make his confession every Friday at 3 p.m. - the time at which it is believed Jesus died on the cross.

He was also very hard on himself in the matter of playing games, even permitted ones like cards and was firm in the necessity of avoiding 'bad or cynical' companions, especially the sort who hang around inns or like to pick a quarrel - presumably, this refers to the vacations! He also warned himself about showing 'too much confidence with women', whether young or old. 'Take the greatest care to guard the stainless lily of purity and to this end keep a close watch on your feelings: guard your eyes especially, never fixing your gaze on a women's face, or on any other source of danger; and beware of eating or drinking too much or between meals and of being idle.'

His warnings and prohibitions are so far from our thinking in the twenty-first century that we instinctively react against them. It is, however, significant that later Angelo also rejected the deprivations demanded by the seminary programme and as priest, bishop and Pope showed an openness which was clearly not inhibited by his early formation. Mgr Ernesto Balducci writes that 'he had a chaste reverence for the reality of the flesh, for its fecundity and even for its instincts'. He was, after all, one of ten children in a farming community. Lawrence Elliott in his biography remarks that 'It was one of the small miracles of the Italian seminary system at the turn of the [nineteenth to the twentieth] century, that young men who had donned the cassock at twelve and had been shut away from the doings of the world for the next decade could still most often emerge as warm and sensitive pastors.'

When he was Papal Nuncio in Paris, a visitor mentioned to him the likelihood of his being made Cardinal and receiving the red hat. 'Hats' said the Nuncio, 'I prefer looking at ladies' hats!' He used to walk about the streets and regularly chatted to the lady who ran the newspaper kiosk where he heard the local news. It is, I think, clear, that his anxieties about contact with women had diminished!

He warned himself in his *Journal* not to be vain about his clothes. He commented later that every stitch he had worn as student and newly ordained priest had been a charitable donation. He frequently accused himself in his *Journal* of talking too much. It is not surprising from what we know of him, as Bishop and Pope, that he was lively, friendly and sociable.

When he was fifteen he wrote that 'My sole object in studying will be to work for the greater glory of God, the honour of the Church, the salvation of souls and not for my own honour'. When he was seventeen he noted in his *Journal*, 'I am convinced of the inestimable worth [of holy purity] and of my own great need of it., as I am called to the angelic ministry of the priesthood....When I am in danger of sinning against holy purity, then more urgently than ever will I appeal

to God, to my Guardian Angel and to Mary with my
familiar invocation, "Mary, Immaculate, help me"...'.
Immaculate, in this context, refers to Mary's coming
into the world without that inherited tendency towards
evil that we call original sin. The next year, 1898, we
read in the *Journal*, 'I thought I would have been a
saint by this time, and instead I am still as miserable as
before....However, I can still thank the Lord for not
having abandoned me as I deserved.'

On Trinity Sunday, he wrote '...I begged Jesus and
Mary for the virtue of humility and I seem to have had
excellent opportunities for exercising it. My Superiors
received an account, I think exaggerated, of my having
behaved arrogantly during the vacation and I have been
duly rebuked.' When he was at home his mother, probably
feeling quite justly, that he was not well fed in the
seminary, would give him little extra bits on his plate,
which aroused the jealousy of others among the nineteen,
who thought he behaved as if receiving the extras was his
right. Some of them had complained to a friar they knew,
who mentioned it to the superior of the seminary. Angelo
was cast down. He wrote 'So I have had to mortify myself
against my will. But, as a matter of fact, there is a grain of
truth in all this. Ah well, if I am now to be out of favour
with my superiors, what am I to do about it?... it...has
given me food for thought and tears...Thanks be to God, I

was never guilty of those excesses, none the less, pride is always present...I have had my lesson.'

The same year, Angelo's family were in difficulties. 'Lord, save us we are perishing. I have had three days of my vacation and already I am tired of it. At the sight of such poverty, in the midst of such suspicions...sometimes I am driven to tears...'

It seems as if a certain jealousy of him, coinciding with worries about the farm and whether it could provide enough resources for them all, provoked a crisis, which Angelo felt keenly. 'At times I think that even those...to whom I have confided all now look at me askance...Ah, how sad that makes me feel! Perhaps I am only imagining this. I hope so...I am suffering when I thought I would be rejoicing.... If Jesus wants my sufferings to continue, his will be done.' Later he wrote 'Oh Jesus, you must look after me a little too.'

He is very hard on himself. 'I really am very greedy about fruit.' Later he wrote 'I have been rather too merry', later adding 'But, after all, it is better to be merry than to be melancholy. And remember "Be glad in the Lord" (*Ps* 31:11)'

In the Holy Year of 1900 he prayed 'Oh most sweet Jesus, accept this little token of my love for you or at least the burning desire I have to love you with all my heart.' His *Journal* records only what he saw as his failures.

To Rome

In 1900 he won a scholarship to the Roman College, but he had barely settled in when, in the following year, he was conscripted into the army - a time he later always referred to as 'The Babylonian Captivity'. Balducci remarks that 'his innocent and terrified eyes had seen many kinds of wickedness the very name of which he had not known before.'

Nevertheless, his army service was an education in itself. It gave him greater understanding of people's difficulties and frailty and he received kindnesses. He wrote to the Rector at the Seminary 'I have excellent officers who make it clear that they like me very much. They...make certain that I have the utmost freedom to fulfil my religious obligations. As for my comrades in the ranks ... I have observed thus far only marks of reverence and affection.' He proved to be a good shot, was promoted to corporal and then just before his demobilisation, was made sergeant.

When he was back in the seminary in Rome, his increasing spiritual and theological maturity began to encourage a more personal view of preparation for priesthood. Rome was an energising cultural experience. He took walks round the city, always with another seminarian, and met many people, students from other colleges, priests, some involved in projects of social development. In his journal for 16 January 1903, he reveals what Balducci calls his 'conversion', a moment of revelation which taught him that the restrictive formation he had endured, was a false path to holiness, at least for him. He wrote in his *Journal*:

'Practical experience has now convinced me of this: the concept of holiness which I had formed and applied to myself was mistaken...in the little failings of which I was aware, I used to call to mind the image of some saint whom I had set myself to imitate down to the smallest particular...However it turned out that I was never able to achieve what I had thought I could do and this worried me. The method was wrong. I must seek holiness ...according to the requirements of my own nature, my own character and the different conditions of my life.'

A few weeks later, he wrote 'serenity and peace', and 'obedience and peace'. These were to be his watchwords. They did not, however, in any way diminish his fervour or make him easy-going in his religious life and he preserved to the end many of the 'little rules' he had set out for himself as a boy.

Living in Rome, he experienced both the beautiful and uplifting ceremonies of the Church and secular pomp and circumstance. The cordiality and ostentation of the reception accorded both to the Prince of Wales and the Emperor of Germany, Protestants both and from countries long hostile to the Church, impressed but saddened him, on their separate visits to Rome. He thought, perhaps wrongly, that it was 'significant', that both saw fit to pay a call on the 'poor old Pope, held like a prisoner in his own house.'

He was deeply moved when he was ordained sub-deacon: 'When, after the solemn prostration, I approached the altar and the Cardinal accepting my vow robed me in my new and glorious habit, it seemed to me that the Popes, confessors and martyrs who sleep in their silent tombs in the basilica rose and embraced me like brothers!'

In retreat before becoming deacon, he confessed to his *Journal* 'It is hard for me to think of a hidden life. I shall be what the Lord wants me to be.' Another entry in 1904 reads 'What will become of me in the future. Shall I be a good theologian or a famous jurist or shall I have a country parish or be just a simple priest.' About the same time, he wrote, '... I find reason for comfort in the words of Jesus to Blessed Margaret Alacoque, "I have chosen you to reveal the marvels of my heart, because you are such an abyss of ignorance and insufficiency". He was deeply aware of his desire to shine and worked hard spiritually to achieve humility and what he calls 'detachment'. He deeply admired Brother Thomas, a Passionist lay brother, who looked after him during his retreat before ordination to the priesthood. 'He is ideally happy... no alluring ambitions, content to be a poor lowly brother for the rest of his life. Before the goodness of Bro. Thomas, I feel my own nothingness; I ought to kiss the hem of his habit and take him for my teacher.'

Ordination to the priesthood

All the years in the seminary brought their reward. Angelo Roncalli was ordained priest in Santa Maria in Monte Santo, Piazza del Popolo on the tenth of August 1904. His *Journal* reads 'When all was over and I raised my eyes, having sworn the oath of eternal fidelity to my Superior, the Bishop, I saw the blessed image of Our Lady, to which I confess I had paid no attention before. She seemed to smile at me and gave me a feeling of sweet peace in my soul and a generous and confident spirit, as if she was telling me she was pleased and would always watch over me...'.

The seminary was empty when he returned, everyone had gone to the country house, Roccantica, belonging to the seminary. He wrote to the Bishop of Bergamo and to his parents, 'begging them to thank the Lord with me'. In the afternoon, he went out and 'utterly absorbed in the Lord, as if there was no-one else in Rome', he visited all his favourite churches, his saints and the loved and familiar images of Our Lady. The following morning, 'my dear Vice-Rector took me to St. Peter's to celebrate my first Mass.' Friends came to the crypt. 'Ah the joys of that Mass!', he wrote. He had most powerful feelings of 'love for the Church, for the cause of Christ, for the Pope and a sense of total dedication to the service of Jesus and the Church ...and [to] unwearying work for souls....I said to the Lord over the tomb of St. Peter, and in his words, "Lord, you know everything; you know that I love you."'

Just about noon that day, Don Angelo Roncalli was taken to an audience with the Holy Father, Pope Pius X, and he told him that 'I was glad to be at his feet repeating to him the intentions I had offered in my first Mass. The Pope bent down, put his hand on his head and almost whispered "Well done, my boy ...this is what I like to hear and I will ask the good Lord ...that you may be a priest after his own heart." Fr. Angelo kissed his hand and he passed on and then turned back and asked when he would be at home. 'I told him for the feast of the Assumption. "Ah, what a feast that will be, up there in your little hamlet...and how those fine Bergamesque bells will peal out on that day," and he continued his round, smiling.'

On August 15th, 'I was at Sotto il Monte; I count that day among the happiest of my life, for me, for my relations and benefactors, for everyone...'. There was great pride and joy among his family and when Don Angelo saw his brothers weeping, his voice broke and he said 'my dear real brothers, seeing you cry in this way unsettles me, though I know they are tears of joy.' After

Mass, an old man offered the 'traditional commendation to a new priest, "Now you must work hard and become Pope!" They both laughed'.

After ordination Don Roncalli restricted the entries in the *Journal of a Soul* to times when he went on retreat. The day-to-day agonising over his spiritual failures was over.

Don Roncalli, Priest

In the Autumn of 1904, his superiors decided that Don Roncalli should study canon law. The euphoria of his ordination was tempered some time later by letters of complaint from his mother. She thought he no longer loved her, he did not write, he had not sent a photograph (though he had sent one to the parish priest); he had sent her no money. He replied: 'Even if I were Pope, you would still remain for me the greatest lady in the world. So please, I beg you don't doubt my love.' He had had to spend his money on new shoes and a soutane for the Mass at Sotto il Monte; books on canon law were very expensive. He would send a photograph when he could, though as he was a simple priest, and no Pope, Cardinal or bishop he did not see why his photograph should be scattered around.

However, his study of canon law was cut short. He was invited by the newly ordained Bishop of Bergamo, Giacomo Radini-Tedeschi, to be his secretary. They had met while Don Roncalli was a student and it seems likely that the future bishop had recognised in him someone whose thinking was on similar lines to his own. Bishop Radini-Tedeschi had been chaplain to the *Opera dei Congressi*, an organisation devoted to social welfare, under Pope Leo XIII. The recently elected Pope Pius X had other priorities and the *Opera dei Congressi* organisation was disbanded, but Radini-Tedeschi was made bishop.

The region of Bergamo had had organisations devoted to social action for many years - Zaverio, Don Roncalli's godfather had been involved in these schemes. It was, therefore, an interesting appointment that Pius X made in sending Radini-Tedeschi, who had been in the forefront of the movement in Rome, to his native Bergamo. Don Roncalli was studying and teaching at the seminary at the same time and he shared with Bishop Radini-Tedeschi a new religious awareness that the sufferings of the poor were not only to be relieved but, as far as possible, removed. The bishop's work with the *Opera dei Congressi* revealed this belief. There were two serious strikes in the Bergamo region at this time, and in each case, he supported the strikers, whose working conditions were very harsh, morally and financially. Don Roncalli knew from personal, family experience the uncertainties and difficulties of poor people, (which the bishop did not), so his warm sympathy would have been of great assistance and provided the bishop with a counter-balance to the criticism he received in some quarters. Priests were usually careful not to become embroiled in political disputes and were expected to remain aloof.

Through his bishop, Roncalli also met the Archbishop of Milan, Cardinal Ferrari, and despite the disparity of rank and age (the Archbishop was fifty-five and Roncalli was twenty-four), they became friends.

St Charles Borromeo

It was through the Cardinal that he came upon the 'Spiritual Archive - Bergamo' of St. Charles Borromeo, thirty nine volumes, relating to the Church in Bergamo soon after the Council of Trent in the sixteenth century. Editing these volumes took many years, and was a labour of love, when he could spare the time from his other work. It was not a frivolous antiquarian interest. St. Charles Borromeo had reformed his diocese, Bergamo again, by the strength of his faith and charity as well as his fervent visits to every parish. Don Roncalli, like St. Charles and Bishop Radini-Tedeschi, wanted every person, by reason of his or her humanity, to be illumined by the Holy Spirit and to work for the greater glory of God. He believed that St. Charles' witness would be invaluable.

Every parish in the diocese, became committed to social as well as religious leadership. The thousands of emigrants, mostly to the U.S.A, were helped with the preparation for their move. The bishop set up three different organisations for the welfare of women, one for women factory workers, one for the protection of young

women and a 'Casa di Maternita' to assist mothers and
their babies. He also set up a working relationship with
the civil authorities - there was no facility at the time for
settling labour disputes - and later unions were permitted.

War

In 1914, Pope Pius X died in distress at the
commencement of the war he had foreseen. A few days
later, Bishop Radini-Tedeschi also died, with Don
Roncalli beside him, to his deep sadness. The conclave
elected Cardinal della Chiesa and he took the name
Benedict XV. In 1915, when Italy entered the war
against Germany and Austria, Don Roncalli was called
up to serve in the army. Priests were now enrolled into
the medical core and he first became an infirmary
assistant. He grew an impressive military-looking
moustache. Years later, he saw a photograph of himself
at that time and remarked 'The moustache was a
mistake. I grew it in a moment of weakness.' In 1916,
the anti-clerical government, having been made aware of
the deeply held faith of many Italians, decreed that
priests should serve as Chaplains to the forces. Years
later, when he was Patriarch in Venice, he wrote, 'How
much I learned about the human heart at this time, how
much experience I gained, how much grace I received to
be able to dedicate myself to the performance of my
duties as military chaplain'. During his retreat in 1919,

he wrote in his *Journal* his sense of the graces that God had granted, giving him numerous occasions for doing good.' He also recorded how 'Many times it happened that I had to throw myself on my knees and weep like a boy, unable any longer to contain the emotion roused by the spectacle of the simple holy deaths of so many poor sons of our people.'

When the war was over, a spirit of optimism swept through Italy. There were some feelings of anxiety in the Church over her relations with the government of Italy, but for the first time since unification, Catholics were permitted by the Church to caste their votes, although the clergy were expected to keep clear of partisan activity. These factors may account for the abrupt changes in the work Don Angelo was required to do. He was first asked by the bishop to open a hostel for students. This was a new idea and Don Roncalli threw himself into it with great enthusiasm, using his own demobilisation grant to help with the furnishing. He loved working with students. However, the very next year, perhaps because of the vigour and his rapport with those he met, he was called to Rome to organise a new centre for missionary activities. The Holy Father wanted him to visit places in France, Belgium and Germany where teaching about, and fund-raising for, the missions were situated. 'You will be God's traveller', Pope Benedict told him. He was made a domestic prelate. The family was impressed, if a little puzzled by his new title. He asked them all to pray for him.

In 1922, Pope Benedict XV died and after many votes in the conclave, Pius XI was elected. As the mood of the country darkened, with both communism and fascism in the ascendant in Italy, 'God's Traveller' continued his efforts to re-organise and promote missionary activity, with the energy of real love for the work.

Two years later, Mgr. Roncalli was appointed Professor of Patristics at the Pontifical Atheneum of the Lateran, a part-time post for which he was well prepared. He clearly relished all his contacts with students. Three months after that, however, he was told to go to Bulgaria as the Pope's representative. It was an abrupt change of direction possibly prompted by his former association with Bishop Radini-Tedeschi, whose fervent advocacy of social action, and its many hints of political involvement, may have frightened the Pontifical Atheneum. However, it had not been a full-time post and he was lost to the successful work for the missions where he had more than doubled the amount of money collected for missionary activities. He was recommended for the post by the head of the congregation for oriental churches, so it may be that he had been spotted as a brilliant and vigorous communicator and a man of humility and faith.

Apostolic visitor to Bulgaria

For Don Angelo Roncalli the appointment to Bulgaria signalled a vast change in his life and work. He did not want to go. He had greatly enjoyed his joint appointments; his two unmarried sisters, whom he had brought to Rome to look after him (and so that he could look after them) were devastated. He had no background in diplomacy. The vast majority of Christians in Bulgaria were Orthodox. Cardinal Gasparri, the Secretary of State told him of his appointment and said that the appointment was an interim one, which would be followed by another that would allow him more scope. Pius XI had decided to ordain Mgr. Roncalli as Archbishop, in order to give him standing in his efforts to improve relations with the Orthodox. 'Obedience and Peace' was his watchword, which he incorporated into his Episcopal coat of arms, and so he went.

There were perhaps sixty thousand catholics in Bulgaria at this time.

By 1925 the country was in turmoil. It had lost much land at the end of the First World War, as an ally of Germany and Austria. There had been an assassination attempt on King Boris and just before the Archbishop's arrival, an ancient Orthodox church had been bombed with many worshippers killed, though the king, who was present, was not hurt. Boris was pleased that the

Apostolic Visitor held the rank of archbishop; he felt it acknowledged the importance of his country.

The Catholics themselves were divided between a majority of Latin rite and a few thousand from Uniate churches whose liturgy was similar to that of the Orthodox, but who accepted the authority of the Pope. Many of the Catholic schools and other institutions in Bulgaria had been set up by French, Swiss or Italian religious orders, which conveyed the impression that the Catholic Church was a foreign institution. Archbishop Roncalli, travelling by cart and donkey visited the distant villages where they mostly lived to encourage them and tell them that he was sent by the Pope to bring them help, where he could.

Humiliations

He realised early on that the Uniates needed a bishop of their own, but it took a year for Rome to give permission. He next asked that a seminary should be set up for both Western and Eastern rites. There was much back and forth about this, but despite Archbishop Roncalli's best efforts, it did not happen. He was deeply disappointed, but he did manage, on his own initiative, to set up a place which provided food for orphans. His journal for 1926, reads, 'As I clearly foresaw, my ministry has brought me many trials. But, and this is strange, these are not caused by the Bulgarians for whom I work, but by the central organs of ecclesiastical administration. This is a form of mortification and humiliation that I did not expect and which hurts me deeply. "Lord you know all".' There was obviously no hope of reconciliation between Orthodox and Catholics. Archbishop Roncalli himself was recognised as being full of good will to all, but he greatly missed pastoral work. 'I never hear confessions', he lamented.

This disappointing state of affairs was intensified in 1930 by a royal marriage. King Boris, who had been baptised and brought up as a Catholic, but was now Orthodox (for reasons of state, rather than conviction), wanted to marry Princess Giovanna, daughter of the king of Italy. The young people genuinely liked each other and it fell to Archbishop Roncalli to explain to the king that the marriage would have to be in a Catholic Church, in accordance with the ordinary rules for mixed marriages. He finally agreed and the marriage took place in Assisi. Six days later, Boris insisted on a further marriage ceremony in the Orthodox church in Sofia. The Archbishop was horrified at Boris' duplicity and some Orthodox themselves were shocked.

Pope Pius blamed Archbishop Roncalli and would not allow him to speak in audience. There were rumours that he might be expelled, but the Pope was determined to keep him there. He elevated his position to that of Apostolate Delegate. Ironically, this pleased King Boris who saw it as a compliment to his country. When his daughter was born, Boris had her baptised in the Orthodox church. Giovanna was powerless, the baby was simply taken to be baptised. Rome thought at the time that Archbishop Roncalli had been too easily taken in. The Archbishop said to the queen that he would tell the Pope that she was blameless and when he did so, the Holy Father believed him. Years later, Pope Pius also realised that he had been unfair to the Archbishop and said to him that as Pope he could not apologise, but 'as *Achille Ratti*, I stand and ask you to pardon me. I give you my hand in friendship.' The Archbishop invited the queen to attend Mass at the Apostolic Delegation, rather than at the main Catholic church to spare her embarrassment.

In 1933, he wrote in his *Journal*, 'My prolonged mission ... in this country often causes me acute and intimate suffering. But I try not to show this; I bear and will bear everything willingly, even joyfully for the love of Jesus in order to resemble him as closely as I can. ... these people so simple and good, but also so unfortunate!' The promises that his time there would be short were not fulfilled. He spent ten years in Bulgaria. His philosophy of acceptance and his natural friendliness of temperament had brought him approval and affection. The Church now needed a new man in Constantinople. The current incumbent had fallen out both with the government and his clergy, and, instructed by Rome, the Archbishop prepared to go under obedience, leaving, he wrote 'with the clear certainty that I have shown everyone that I love them in the Lord...'

Apostolic Delegate in Istanbul

Archbishop Roncalli made his first appearance in the cathedral at Constantinople, newly renamed Istanbul, on the feast of the Epiphany. His face, recorded the French archivist of the delegation, was 'radiant with kindness'. He said that he had loved the Bulgarians, but now his heart opens 'like arms and leans toward you who are to form my new spiritual family'.

There were some thirty five thousand Catholics out of a population of around eighteen million. Kemal Ataturk, determined to make Turkey an 'up-to-date' nation, was opposed both to Islam and Christianity. Archbishop Roncalli's diplomatic role had no status with the government, which, he claimed, freed him to look after his flock but soon after his arrival, there was a prohibition on clerical dress. He took it philosophically. 'If in Rome, Christ is a Roman, let him be a Turk in Turkey!' He even showed his staff how to tie neck-ties. 'I learned it in the army', he said with, possibly, some satisfaction. He re-assured them: 'it isn't death or imprisonment.'

He was anxious that Catholics should know that it was possible to be a good Catholic and a good Turk. He also discerned that strong opposition to secularization might kill off the whole Catholic community. As in Bulgaria, he promoted the use of the local language for the reading of the Gospel, his own sermons and the Divine Praises, though his first sermon was in French. He worried deeply about the future of the fine Catholic schools which existed in Istanbul, but without diplomatic status he was unable to make protests to the government. After he was elected Pope, the Turkish government requested regular and permanent diplomatic contacts with the Holy See.

In July that year, 1935, the Archbishop received the sad news of his father's death. He went to the chapel and cried 'like a child'. One of his great joys had been to pass his holidays as priest and bishop at Sotto il Monte, spending time with his father on the land. He was unable to attend the funeral, because of the tense situation in Istanbul. He knew well that his father had been proud of his bishop son and he tried to console his mother with the thought of the many Masses and prayers that would be offered for his father, including a beautiful and imposing Mass that he would celebrate in his cathedral. When he got back to Sotto il Monte for the holidays, he took his mother by car to visit the shrines of Our Lady that they both loved. He arranged for her to move to his house in the village, where his sisters Ancilla and Maria were now living and could devote time to her away from the bustle of the family home. After his father's death he wrote personally to her far more frequently. His mother herself died in 1939 of influenza. The great joy of her widowed life had been his holiday visits and letters. She knew he came and wrote when he could. As with his father, he was not able to attend her funeral, which took place just before the conclave that elected Pope Pius XII.

Greece

Archbishop Roncalli was also Apostolic Delegate to Greece. Here too he encountered obstacles in the way. His predecessor had been denied a visa, possibly because he had been insufficiently tactful, but Roncalli was given a visa for eight days, without diplomatic privileges. Once again, he was working in a country that was beginning to modernise itself, but was also turning away from religion. Greece was near to having a dictatorship. The Archbishop was determined to travel widely, but without pomp. Little by little, he managed to visit many of the Orthodox monasteries, including Mount Athos. His Christian openness, his eagerness to learn and his friendly manner disarmed the wary. Roncalli knew that his work would not bring much in the way of results. He described it as 'Ant's work, bee's work'.

The entry of Italy into the war on the side of the Axis, on July 10 1940 was a terrible day for the Archbishop. His Episcopal chancellor was French, and Archbishop Roncalli received him the next day. He gave him the kiss of peace and unable to trust himself to improvise, read what he had written. '...[War] is an iniquity and contradiction...I must be the bishop of all, that is the *consul dei*, God's consul, father, light, encouragement for all....grace fills me more than ever with the desire to seek and work for peace.' In his *Journal* he wrote 'I am a teacher of mercy and truth', not, he explains, of political science or human knowledge. 'Words move, but examples draw.'

The Greeks were defeated and occupied. They were reduced to near starvation. Roncalli alerted the Vatican and money and goods were sent, but more was needed than the Vatican was able to supply. He begged German and Italian consuls and others to apply to get food to Greece. Rumania and Hungary sent help. The Vatican set up a centre for tracing prisoners of war and the Apostolic Delegation acted as a clearing house for enquiries from Syria, Palestine and Egypt. The Archbishop also contrived to assist thousands of Jews from Slovakia by providing them with visas for Palestine, but his room for action was pitiably small. The best he could do was to forward to the Vatican diplomats in Hungary and Rumania 'Immigration Certificates' issued by the Palestine Jewish agency which in a good number of cases facilitated the emigration of Jews from those countries. After the war, this gave rise to the unfounded belief in some circles that the Archbishop has issued certificates of baptism. In December 1944, he was unexpectedly asked to go to Paris as Nuncio, the representative of the Pope. He accepted on the grounds that he must not refuse any work he was asked to do.

Nuncio to France

Mgr. Valerio Valeri had been Nuncio to France for eleven years, through the changes of government in those tumultuous time, including the years of German occupation. De Gaulle as President, wanted a replacement, but Pius XII would not accede to the President's wish, for fear that it would look as if Mgr. Valeri had been too close to the Vichy government. For some months, there was no Nuncio. New Year was approaching and the Nuncio traditionally presented greetings to the Head of State on behalf of the *Corps Diplomatique*. If there was no Nuncio, the Russian ambassador would have the honour. The Pope himself therefore hurriedly decided to appoint Archbishop Roncalli and he arrived in Paris at the end of 1944, just in time to present the New Year greetings to the President and into the maelstrom of anxiety and uncertainty that resulted from the years of occupation. The war had created a deep divide among French people and the Church was inevitably affected. Some seven bishops were asked to resign on the grounds that they had, at least initially, been too close to the Vichy

regime. This was to some extent a sop to the new
government: the Vichy regime had been a legitimate
one. The bishops went honourably, with pensions but
without fuss. At the same time, there was great
intellectual and spiritual vigour among the religious
orders and others in France.

There was also an initiative new to the Church; that of
Worker Priests. Priests taken by the Nazis for forced
labour alongside lay people had developed strong
empathy with the problems of workers. Some wished to
continue this solidarity in order to re-Christianise urban
working people by being with them in factories and
fitting their priestly life around their work. The Cardinal
Archbishop of Paris permitted and upheld the project,
although many Catholics objected. The Nuncio had to
pass on the objections to Rome. He had a natural
sympathy with the difficulties of the poor and was
burningly aware of the need for effective catechesis and
spiritual sustenance. He also treasured the proper
demands of priesthood. As Nuncio, he had only to report.
Cardinal Ottaviani, the Secretary of State to the Holy
Father, felt that priests would be unable to fulfil their
spiritual duties while working in this way.

In a speech in 1956, the Nuncio told an anecdote
about a worker priest. Some workmen said to this good
honest priest, as they donned their overalls, "This is no
place for you. Here is a bit of spare ground; we will help

you to build a chapel hut. We will bring our wives and children to it and who knows? Perhaps we will come too. This is what we want from you: your Gospel and your altar, nothing else." The men in this story had the rights of it. Ultimately, the movement could not hold and Pope John gently suggested to the French cardinal, Feltin, that concern for the integrity of priesthood, which was paramount, should not be seen as pushing workers away.

Archbishop Roncalli was not temperamentally attuned to theological speculation of the kind that was enlivening the French Church during these years. He remarked to a Jesuit that he wished that Teilhard de Chardin would be content with the Catechism and social teaching, 'instead of bringing up all these problems,' - though this may have been a joke. In 1950, Pope Pius XII defined the doctrine of the Assumption of Our Lady. It had, in fact, been a general belief of Catholics since the Middle Ages and the definition of the Immaculate Conception of Mary (her own conception free from that tendency towards evil that derives from original sin) almost required it as a corollary. The Archbishop had certainly held it since his youth. The Pope's act may be thought to have startled and even issued a warning to some theologians, including those in France, that the definition of doctrine did not lie with the theologians alone. The Archbishop's own intellectual interests resided in ecclesiastical history and a

Nuncio had other duties which referred not to the Church *per se*, but to relations between Church and state.

The Nuncio got on well with the President of France and facilitated the ongoing discussions about funding of Catholic schools. They were not finally completed, but Catholic schools received some aid from the Government. He wanted to be sure that the old hostility between Church and government would not arise again. He also accepted the post of Vatican observer to UNESCO and believed fervently that the interests of justice and peace, culture and liberty, should be upheld by all nations. He saw that the good in all human situations and endeavours could be used for the greater glory of God.

In 1952, Archbishop Roncalli was made Cardinal. 'It's not a sacrament, not even a sacramental', he said. The very same day he heard that his sister Ancilla who had looked after him and their mother, was dying of cancer. He had been asked if he would accept the appointment of Patriarch of Venice after the death of the present incumbent. He was to keep it secret at that time. He wrote in his *Journal*; 'I prayed and thought about it and answered "Obedience and Peace". I remember St. Joseph and follow his example. So I push my donkey off in a new direction and bless the Lord.' This appointment, above all, he must have relished. He was to be a parish priest writ large.

Patriarch of Venice

Returning to Italy must have been a delight to Cardinal
Roncalli, in itself. His French had never been of a quality
to take on sophisticated and speculative Parisian
Catholics and to be back to the place where his language
was common parlance was a real pleasure. The history
that absorbed him had taken place near at hand. Bergamo
was not so far from Venice and as the Cardinal said
Bergamo had 'formed the character of our peoples on the
pattern of Venice.' His desire to work as a pastor was
fulfilled and in his first speech to the Venetian people, he
said 'I want to talk to you with the greatest
frankness....Things have been written about me that
greatly exaggerated my merits. I ... have an inclination to
love people.... It stops me doing harm to anyone; it
encourages me to do good to all.... I come from Bergamo,
land of St. Mark'. Venetians warmed to him and his
evident desire to stress what unites people rather than
the things that divide them. On another occasion, he
said '... From my birth I have never wanted to be
anything but a priest. Thus the humble son of the people
was granted a wonderful mission that was to be for the
people's good. ... He is able to carry out this task
because he himself feels the weight of human
frailty...When you look at your Patriarch, look for the
priest... the pastor... A man of little worth, a humble

priest, but above all a shepherd. I shall get to know you all, but simply, without ceremony, with swift and silent steps.' He understood priesthood as service, first of God and second of men and women.

He was saddened by the contrasts in Venice, the beauty and splendour, the poverty and misery. He did not have much money himself and was constantly dismayed by requests for help. On the other hand, he did not want to be a rich prelate. He was keen for workers to be properly paid and was aware that their leaders tended to be communists or socialists, both of whom were hostile to the Church. He was, however, prepared to take their sincere concerns for the welfare of working people at face value and therefore when the Socialist Party Congress was held in Venice, the Cardinal welcomed it. Endorsement from the communist press, however, created something of a scandal. People were loath to believe that Cardinal Roncalli meant what he said. He was not preparing to be a socialist: he was acknowledging that socialists could honestly desire what they thought was best for workers. He believed, with some justice, that his calm and kindly approach had reduced the hostility between the Socialists and the Church.

He also wanted to re-vitalise the Archdiocese. He was not simply a naturally kind and friendly man. He passionately wanted the life of Christ to be present in every individual. He began by visiting many parishes.

Then he wanted to bring together the bishops and priests. His life's literary and historical work was on St. Charles Borromeo's campaign to sanctify the ordinary people of Bergamo in his time (the sixteenth century). St. Charles had called a synod. Bishop Radini-Tedeschi, 'his' bishop, had called a synod. Archbishop Roncalli would follow them.

He described the synod in a letter to the Venetians: 'You've probably heard the word *aggiornamento*... Well, Holy Church who is ever youthful wants to be in a position to understand the diverse circumstances of life, so that she can adapt, correct, improve and be filled with fervour.' Did that mean that he wanted doctrinal innovations? There is no evidence that it did. The 'bringing up to date' required a continuous seeking for a way to express eternal truths so that people in general could more easily respond to them. By gentle methods, Cardinal Roncalli brought new animation to the Church in Venice.

In 1961, a reception was given for Pope John on his eightieth birthday. Talking to family members, he said that when he was Patriarch of Venice, he was very happy and he went on: 'Then the Pope died and I went to Rome for the conclave and I said to myself "Angelo, they wouldn't, would they?" But they did.'

THE UNIVERSAL PARISH PRIEST

On October 9th, 1958, Pius XII died and the next day Cardinal Roncalli took the train from Venice to Rome for his funeral. The Pope had been greatly admired for his evident holiness and his clear intelligence. The recent history of the papacy, and the terrible years of the war had isolated him, while the last years of his papacy had been damaged by his ill-health, but there were no serious signs of the hostility and denigration, which appeared considerably later. In his *Journal*, Cardinal Roncalli wrote when he heard of the Pope's death 'Pius XII is in Paradise'.

He set off at once for Rome for the funeral. There are traditionally nine days of official mourning for a Pope and the Conclave was to start on October 25th. The time up to a conclave provides an opportunity for the Cardinals to speak among themselves in order to learn about each others' particular concerns and the ways in which these would produce a sketch of the next pope. Pius XII had created an electoral college which, for the first time, was not mostly Italian. He had himself reigned for nineteen years. The Cardinals spoke together about whether an old Pope and a short reign would be more desirable than a younger Pope, who would probably be in place much longer.

Papal election

The conclave produced a number of votes. At first no candidate dominated, but as they progressed, it became clear that Cardinal Roncalli's name was appearing more and more on the ballot papers. On October 28th, Cardinal Roncalli, who, of course, understood the position, celebrated Mass at six in the morning. Then he served Mgr. Capovilla's Mass (he was his secretary). The cardinals had breakfast in haste and then went to the Sistine chapel for Mass. They sang the *Veni Creator*. The votes were still moving towards Cardinal Roncalli, though the margin necessary was not yet achieved. He himself stayed upstairs in his room. Mgr. Capovilla recalled that he went in to bring him down for lunch, but he wanted to stay in his room and asked that something be brought up so that they could eat together. Some soup, a slice of meat, a glass of wine and an apple were provided. The two of them ate at a little table and found it hard to talk. The Cardinal rested for some twenty minutes and then sat at the desk to make notes for the acceptance speech, he now knew he would have to make. He came down for the eleventh ballot and received thirty-eight of the possible fifty one votes, more than the two thirds needed. He wrote in his diary that he asked his favourite saints 'to give me calmness and courage'. When he was elected he prayed the psalm "Have mercy on me Lord, in thy great mercy."

He accepted the decision of the conclave. He was asked what name he would be known by and he replied 'I will be called John'. He explained that John was his father's name and the church where he was baptised was dedicated to St. John. John was the name of the two men closest to Our Lord, 'John the Baptist and John the Apostle and Evangelist.' He remarked that John had been the name of more Popes than any other and he added, mischievously, 'Most of them had a short reign!' He repeated St. John's continuous injunction 'Love one another.'

Arrayed in a white cassock, which proved to be too small and had to be held together with safety pins, hidden by his surplice, Pope John gave his first blessing as Pope. There had been a farcical moment when the Pope had asked Guido Gusso, his chauffeur and general factotum, to go to his lodging to bring him back some shoes (the Papal ones provided did not fit.) With some difficulty, he managed to get out and as the door opened a crowd of prelates and helpers of the various cardinals rushed in, to be greeted by a furious Cardinal Tisserant, who shouted, 'The conclave is not finished, you are all excommunicated.' When Pope John was told of this fracas, he said mildly, 'Well, we shall have to use our influence to absolve these unfortunates.'

His family heard the news on the radio, with amazement! He wrote in his diary, 'About three hundred thousand people applauded me on St. Peter's balcony. The arc-lights stopped me from seeing anything other than a shapeless, heaving mass. I blessed Rome and the world as if I were a blind man.' Later on he added, '... I said to myself, if you don't remain a disciple of the gentle and humble Master you'll understand nothing... Then you'll be really blind.'

That night, he did not sleep but prayed. He wrote; 'It was such a burden; I never felt such a weight. But the Lord wished it... Today the whole world is talking about me, my name and myself. O Mama, O Father, Grandfather, Uncle Zaverio, where are you? Who brought us to such honour? Pray for me.' His secretary, Mgr. Capovilla told how in the night John decided to face his fears and have a word with the Pope. Then he realised he was the Pope and said aloud 'Very well, I will speak to the Lord God about it.'

His coronation was arranged for the feast of St. Charles Borromeo, whose re-energising work for the Church in Bergamo had for many years been an inspiration to Pope John. His family all came, proud and anxious. They had places near the papal throne during the Mass. When they had first arrived, they were tongue-tied with embarrassment, but as soon as they met Pope John, they were happy. They noted he was just the same, loving, full of little jokes, able to put them at their ease. Some of them wept and he said 'Don't cry. It's not so bad what they have done to me!' As Pope, he was determined that his family should stay the same. He helped them all, in their various needs, but was certain that they should not obtain great material advantages because of their relationship to him.

Setting a precedent, the Pope preached a homily at the end of the solemn and grand Coronation Mass. Despite the grandeur of the occasion, he spoke, to the assembled prelates, clergy and the wider world, of the Pope as a shepherd, as one like Joseph in the Old Testament, who met his brothers again and simply said to them 'I am Joseph, your brother.' He was to be a Pope in a way that accorded both with his temperament and his deep faith, just as, when he was young, he had come to realise that he could not attain holiness by imitating others, who were different from him in their personalities and talents.

Character

Pope John was decisive about the things that he wanted. He told the editor of the Vatican paper *Osservatore Romano* that he was to cut out the flowery phrases that were customary to describe the Pope. He hated solitary meals, and remarked that he had searched Holy Scripture and found nothing that said that the Pope had to eat alone! Thereafter he often invited friends and visitors to lunch or dine with him. His new coat of arms interested him. It incorporated the Lion of St. Mark, as a reference to his time as Patriarch. He was worried by the original

sketch, because he thought the lion looked too fierce. He
said he wanted a more human lion. He liked to walk in
the Vatican gardens and did not want the tourists
banished. 'I promised I won't do anything to scandalise
them', he said. He liked to chat to the gardeners. They
had been instructed to disappear when Pius XII walked in
the garden, but Pope John changed that. Talking to the
men about their families and living conditions, he found
out that the Holy See paid very low wages and without
further consultation, he raised them to near commercial
levels. Justice was of prime importance to him and he
knew a lot about poverty at first hand. The Vatican
treasury was worried that it would empty the coffers. In
fact, Pope John's popularity was such that many more
pilgrims came, thereby increasing the treasury income.

He also liked to get out of the Vatican and visit sick
friends and others. Then he inaugurated visits to parishes,
often those in poor districts, on Sundays. 'The Pope's
greeting is always this *Pax vobiscum*'. On one occasion,
he went on 'These visits outside the Vatican are a great
joy to me. The Pope is a recluse in his great palace; all
the world comes to see him, but ... he lives in two or three
rooms at most, all enclosed. Let the Pope come out a
little... to inspire you with Christian ideals and to help us
all in our sacrifices.'

He would go out quite spontaneously, without the two
hours' notice, he was supposed to give to alert the Swiss

Guard and others. On his first Christmas as Pope, he went, after Mass, to visit the children's hospital, the Gesu Bambino, without warning anyone. To a little boy who said his name was Angelo, he said, 'We used to be called Angelo once'. On St. Stephen's Day, he went to the Regina Coeli prison. 'You could not come to me', he said to the prisoners, 'so I came to you. Are you glad I came?' He then told them about a relative of his who had been in prison for hunting without a license. *'Viva Il Papa'*, they shouted. He demanded to be taken into the part where serious offenders were kept. He said to them 'I have pressed my heart against yours.' A convicted murderer fell on his knees and called out 'Can there be forgiveness for someone like me?' Pope John lifted him to his feet and embraced him.

He made visits to many parishes and was received with enormous enthusiasm, but he insisted on his teaching role, telling cheering congregations to listen to his words, and not just shout, however affectionately.

The great plan

As Bishop of Rome, he wanted to be a real pastor to his diocese and beyond. In his diary, Pope John recorded his announcement to Cardinal Tardini of his proposed Council of all the bishops of the Church, including all the rites in union with Rome and bishops from every part of the world.

On the feast of the Conversion of St. Paul, the Pope travelled to the church of St. Paul's Outside the Walls to announce his plan to the Cardinals in Rome. There were to be three major events: a synod of the Diocese of Rome; an Ecumenical Council and a revision of the Code of Canon Law. He said his decision was based on the tradition of the Church, who had enjoyed periods of renewed clarity in her thought, which served to strengthen her holiness and emphasise her unity. As Bishop of Rome, he wished to encourage the priests of the diocese, as he had done in Venice. Before declaring that there would be an ecumenical Council, he had said to his secretary, 'Christ has been there on the cross with his arms out-stretched for two thousand years. Where have we got to in proclaiming the Good News?' The press statement announcing the Council said that it was intended, not only for Christians, but as an invitation 'to separated communities to search for the unity to which so many souls in all parts of the world aspire.'

The Cardinals listened to him without apparent enthusiasm. Pope John was deeply disappointed. But later the mood changed and many positive letters arrived, expressing excitement and hope. Among the most positive was that of Cardinal Montini, a friend and colleague who shared many of his ideas. He wrote in a pastoral letter to his diocese of Milan 'A flame of enthusiasm swept over the whole Church.' The Holy

Father himself sat back from arrangements for the Council, having decided that freedom for the participants was a necessity for success. It was also axiomatic that the Curia would be less thrilled than the bishops since it was most likely that the prelates from all over the world would have criticisms of the way in which the Church was governed from Rome. Each one would probably have a particular complaint or disappointment. In April 1959, the Holy Father addressed representatives of Catholic universities and outlined his hopes for the Council. 'By giving an admirable view of the cohesion, unity and concord of the holy Church of God, a city set upon a mountain, [it] will, of itself, constitute an invitation to our separated brothers, who bear the honourable name of Christians, to return to the universal flock whose direction it was the changeless wish of Christ to confide to St. Peter.' His best hope probably lay with the Orthodox, who share the essence of Catholic belief, and whose separation John believed came more from political than theological causes. His time in Bulgaria had taught him much about Orthodoxy.

In the meantime, the Roman synod took place in January 1960. It lasted only three days and the Holy Father, as Bishop of Rome, addressed them himself. He was concerned that priests should behave in ways that revealed their priesthood at all times, as he demanded of himself in his *Journal*. He also urged charity and friendship to priests who had left the priesthood or were under censure. In earlier times, such men had been left to sink or swim. He believed that synods served to assist the clergy, aware that the dedication and holiness of priests 'leavened' the whole of a diocese and could transform the faith of the people of God in that place.

In the Council, unlike the Synod, discussion was to be paramount. When preparatory commissions were set up to prepare for the Council, senior members of the Curia, whatever their reservations, were involved in each one, along with other bishops and advisers. Pope John himself made a clear distinction between the job of the Curia (that is, the government of the Church) and the Council. The Council was to think freely about the Church's mission. By November 1960, the preparatory commissions were ready to begin work, having received two thousand letters detailing matters of concern. They were to be guided by a central commission, with the Pope at its head, and with the new Secretariat for Christian Unity to assist with explorations of other Christian denominations and by other commissions on important subjects. The Holy Father told all those involved that he wanted to show the Church as she should be and thereby to reveal 'the quality of human and Christian life, of which the Church is the custodian and mistress throughout the centuries.'

The new Secretariat for Christian Unity, under an elderly but vigorous Jesuit, Cardinal Augustine Bea, was set up in order both to achieve a better understanding of Protestant denominations and to explain the Catholic position to them. There was to be 'no question at all of adopting their outlook or their faith', the Cardinal said in an address that was later published. But they were, after all, baptised Christians and shared the beliefs of Catholics on The Trinity, and Christ's redemptive act, as well as the Ten Commandments. Protestants were not in any usual sense personally culpable for being Protestants. They had been born into it and for many it was a faith that they followed with love and care. The Archbishop of Canterbury when he was about to visit the Holy Father in December 1960, took a more acerbic approach. He preached a sermon in the Anglican church in Rome, in which he proclaimed that the collegial structure of the Church of England most resembled the admirable 'unity and diversity' of the British Commonwealth! The monarchical system of the Church of Rome, on the other hand, could lead straight to dictatorship. Archbishop Fisher could not foresee the travails of a Church without authority, which have come upon the Church of England since the later years of the twentieth century. He told Pope John, it is said, that the idea that the Church of the Apostles subsisted uniquely in the Catholic Church was old hat and that the churches ran in two parallel lines, which will 'merge in eternity'. Pope John's report of the meeting recorded that they talked of St. Augustine's mission to Canterbury in 597 A.D.

However, the visit did represent a breakthrough to better personal relations between Catholics and Protestants.

The Holy Father spoke of the functions that he intended the forthcoming Council to fulfil. First of all, he spoke of *aggiornamento*, a bringing up-to-date of the Church's way of communicating her mission. An 'Ecumenical Council' is one that comprises the whole Catholic Church. It does not necessarily imply a coming together of different Christian communities not in union with Rome. The fruit of this meeting, he hoped, would be a clearer understanding of the Church by the 'separated brethren', (that is Christians, separated from Mother Church) which in turn would make their 'return' easier. He softened this term in his first encyclical, by adding ... we do not invite you to some strange house, but to your own, shared paternal home...I am Joseph your brother.' The quotation from Genesis was a significant and favourite one of his, signifying his brotherhood as man as well as his fatherhood as Pope. Later on, shortly before the Council, he used vaguer language, praying for the return 'to unity and peace'. In his mind, a still wider concern was becoming clearer. It was the belief that the Council would enlighten and encourage all mankind. It was also his belief that the ordinary, social and material well-being of all men was also the concern of the Church. He spoke of himself as the '... father of the whole human family, which God has entrusted to me'.

Mater et Magistra

As the Council preparations continued, he published one of his two most important and striking encyclicals, *Mater et Magistra*. He opens it by saying that 'Christianity ... lays claim to the whole man, body and soul, intellect and will, inducing him to raise his mind above the changing conditions of this earthly existence' and yet 'the Church concerns herself with the exigencies of man's daily life', livelihood, education, 'temporal welfare and prosperity.' The occasion was the seventieth anniversary of Pope Leo XIII's great encyclical, known as *Rerum Novarum* (literally 'Of New Things', that is, the idea of social development and the condition of working people.) Pope John was himself very open and even enthusiastic about 'new things'. He endorsed the teaching of Leo XIII that payment for work cannot be left exclusively to the state of the market, and justice must be applied. Nevertheless, he defended private property as a 'natural right', but at the same time he taught that governments had a duty to promote the common good by institutions and laws.

The encyclical is essentially an optimistic document. It celebrates the increased numbers and influence of unions, co-operatives and associations of all kinds, as ways of working for the common good. He speaks of the rights of workers to have a say in the running of companies and even a share in the profits. He sees a government's function as that of furthering the welfare of the people while employing the principle of subsidiarity (that decisions should be taken locally, as far as possible). Subsidiarity inhibits governments from taking too much power and 'micro-managing' the life of the nation. Men need, he stresses, and have both the right and duty to be primarily responsible for their own upkeep and that of their families. He rejects class warfare and remarks that tyranny ensues when people have no room for personal initiatives. He writes from the heart, especially about the difficulties of those who live in the countryside. He had known their sorrows all his life. He sets out the need for infra-structure, advocates credit unions with lower rates of interest that farmers would be able to afford, and also proper price protection as they waited for harvest.

The countryside, he writes is 'rich in allusions to God the Creator and Provider' and work there 'carries a dignity all its own.' It is interesting that many of Pope John's ideas were put, at least partially, into practice by Christian Democrat ministers in certain European countries.

'We are all equally responsible for the undernourished peoples', he writes and he rejoices to see help going from the rich to the poor nations. At the same time, he insists that it is essential to avoid any type of neo-colonialism, which would ignore indigenous cultures. The Church, however, is not foreign anywhere and she is 'perennially youthful'. He was deeply saddened by the persecution of Christians, wherever it occured.

The pressure for some form of population control, which was a mark of the time, he rejects as being against man's existential dignity and he points out that problems are caused by deficient economic and social organisations. Moves against human dignity result in materialism and loss of freedom. Respect for marriage and families is necessary and new life reveals 'the creating hand of God.' Children need to be given proper religious formation along with food and shelter, since the moral order has no existence except in God.

Christians must adhere to their principles and follow the Church's teaching, but also be generous to others. 'The Universal Pastor of Souls', as he describes himself, is 'heavy of heart' when he sees the growing secularisation of the Lord's Day. 'The laity must increase and intensify their Christian commitment'. Even in daily work, and he quotes St. Paul, we can '... do all for the glory of God.' The encyclical was well liked and understood as a new opening to the world.

Global anxieties

Meanwhile the preparations for the Council were continuing and the Holy Father was approaching his eightieth birthday. During his summer visit to Castel Gandolfo he wrote, most touchingly, in his *Journal* that 'this life of mine, now nearing its sunset, could find no better end than in the concentration of all my thoughts in Jesus, the Son of Mary, who holds him out to me in her arms for the joy and comfort of my soul.' He continued, 'I shall go on trying to perfect my pious practices...,' reflecting what has been called his 'fidelity to childhood' - simple practices he had used all his life and which, after his Council, have been so often neglected or minimized.

The serenity of his spiritual life was in contrast to the global anxieties of the time, though, of course, he was aware of them and shared them. He realised, as well, that he had a huge programme before him in preparing and carrying through his largest enterprise, the Council. He seems from his Journal to have been quite amused that the Cardinals, who thought they were electing a provisional and transitory Pope, were now looking at one in the fourth year of his pontificate, with his greatest work before him, old as he was! With humility, he saw a 'reason for shame at my own littleness and worthlessness.' While the Berlin wall was being built and America and Russia were increasingly at odds, preparations for the Council were quickening.

Kruschev sent a telegram congratulating Pope John on his eightieth birthday, as a token of his work for peace. He responded and on the back of this innovative exchange later sent special invitations to the Catholic bishops who were mostly in the Baltic States, under Russian rule, to attend the Council. What was the Council intended to achieve? This was a question that was in the minds of all connected with it. The pope himself left it to the Central Preparatory Commission, while acknowledging proposals he liked. It was not to be a vehicle for condemnations. It was to be optimistic, believing that the Holy Spirit would guide its endeavours. It was to re-connect faith with the world and to teach all people about the love of God in Christ. There was already much interest among the Protestant churches. A Catholic bishop from East Germany suggested terms to be avoided in writing of the 'church of silence' - that phrase itself being the first of them. He pointed out that language had to be conciliatory, if Catholics were to be helped. Such discretion did not imply a pro-communist position.

Politics again dampened hopes of progress with the Orthodox at this point. The Patriarchs disagreed among themselves about their response to the invitation to attend the Council, so that the Patriarch of Constantinople, who was personally enthusiastic, and had therefore been approached by Rome as representative of Orthodoxy, felt that he could not accept unilaterally. The Patriarch of Moscow, on the other hand, held that individual invitations should have been sent to each of the Patriarchs. Thus it was that, because of the Moscow Patriarch's view, a separate invitation was addressed to him with the result that two Russian orthodox priests came to the Council, but no others.

Cardinal Suenens said in his tribute to the Holy Father after his death that Pope John was one day in the gardens of Castel Gandolfo, reading the preparatory texts, when he said to the Cardinal; 'I know what my personal part in the preparation of the Council will be....It will be suffering.' He already expected sickness and death.

The Council opens - October 11th, 1962

The Pope prepared for the Council with a retreat and saw it in prospect as an opportunity for the Church to proclaim the cry that 'echoes down the centuries from Bethlehem, *Pacem in Terris*, Peace on Earth'. The Church was to look at herself and judge how far she reflected Christ's mandate, "Go and teach all nations".

Before the Council met, the Holy Father, on the advice of his doctors, had X-rays and other diagnostic investigations. His Secretary described the results as life-threatening, but they were not made public. Pope John with his usual serenity decided to make a pilgrimage to Loreto and Assisi. In the latter place he spoke of the 'coming together of earth and heaven', which he foresaw as the goal of the Council.

The bishops started to arrive from all corners of the world. There could be no doubt that the Church was Catholic and therefore 'universal'; the bishops, most of them dressed in the purple, were themselves ethnically diverse, coming from Africa, Asia, including China and

India, the Middle East, as well as from Europe, including some from Eastern Europe, North and South America and Oceania. The Council opened on 11 October 1962 with Holy Mass celebrated by Cardinal Tisserant. The Holy Father spoke at the end of Mass, after reading out the profession of faith, which was repeated on behalf of the bishops. He told them that this Council was not to be a condemnation of things that were wrong, nor was it to be a simple repetition of the teaching of past councils or the magisterium. He said it was to be a deeper 'doctrinal penetration' using contemporary vocabulary and methods of research. Pope John wished to spread and deepen the faith in the most effective way. Years later, Pope John Paul II stated that the Council 'stands in continuity with the faith of all times...'.

The Holy Father's unshakeable and natural optimism and his acceptance of the modern world, shone through his words. He almost made fun of the 'prophets of doom' whom he encountered, he said, 'in the everyday exercise of our pastoral ministry'. He believed that 'today Providence is guiding us towards a new order of human relationships which ... can lead to the good of the Church.'

The human response to Pope John XXIII was overwhelming. The crowds filled St. Peter's Square with confident joy in their hearts. The Pope appeared at his window to shouts of love and excitement. Characteristically, he found just the right words. 'Even the moon', he said, 'has hurried out' to watch. His voice, as he claimed, echoed the voice of the world. He told his hearers to go back home and give their children a kiss from the Pope.

The Cold War intervenes

Nine days later, America and Russia were threatening nuclear attacks over the long-range missiles which Russia had sent to Cuba. Soviet ships were going in the same direction. A journalist, Norman Cousins, editor of the *Saturday Review*, discussed the position with two Russians who happened to be at a scientific conference in the United States at that time. It was clear that neither side could back down without serious loss of face. The journalist brought together the Russians and a priest and suggested that the Pope might be able to defuse the situation if he called publicly for peace. The Russians who had good Kremlin contacts, alerted Khruschev. The priest, Fr. Morhain contacted the Vatican and his message was given to the Holy Father. He at once agreed to do what he could and added to a scheduled talk (to Portuguese pilgrims) words addressed to the world leaders, praying that they would listen 'to the anguished cries... from innocent babies to the old, "peace, peace"'. There was at that time, no presumption of peace; the Russian threat to the West had succeeded Nazi aggression. At his Wednesday weekly audience, the Holy

Father said that the efforts of statesmen to avoid war and bring peace from whatever side, always had the endorsement of the Pope. He also sent a message to the Russian embassy in Rome begging 'heads of state not to remain insensitive to the cry of humanity, peace, peace.' His cry for peace was broadcast by Vatican radio. The Russian government-controlled newspaper, *Pravda*, published it prominently, which was a sign that Khruschev saw the Pope's intervention as a way out. Soon afterwards, half of the Soviet fleet turned back from Cuba. President Kennedy was grateful to the Pope, knowing he had been let off the hook. Khruschev asked for moves towards disarmament and acknowledged the part Pope John had played. Hebblethwaite, in his biography, attributes the first move in this to Kennedy himself. He also notes that there are no references to it in the biographies of the President, perhaps because of the sensitivities attached to the first Catholic Presidency of the United States.

What were the subjects that touched the men and women of those years most closely? The Pope believed that peace and the fear of war were the closest to their hearts. During the Cuban missile crisis, he had been at the centre of the tension and his secretary, Mgr. Capovilla, dates the idea of his last encyclical, *Pacem in Terris*, to that time.

The Council gets down to work

The Council continued its deliberations slowly, revealing painful divisions between the bishops 'in the world' and the dicasteries (departments) of the Vatican. Pope John did not intervene though he watched many of the proceedings on closed circuit television. During the first debate which was on the liturgy, the Holy Father, during his homily at Mass, made the point that the Ambrosian rite was the closest to the original Roman rite and it had come from Milan. The rite of the washing of the feet on Maundy Thursday also derived from the practice of Milan. This was a hint that the liturgy could be re-shaped and, perhaps, a nod in the direction of his close friend. Cardinal Montini, Archbishop of Milan and his successor as Pope Paul VI.

He sent an occasional mark of esteem to a bishop whose contribution pleased him particularly. The Archbishop of Cambrai, or instance, was sent a present of his Venetian writings, after a speech in which he highlighted the importance of re-stating truths attractively but without glossing over hard-to-accept doctrines. On November 10, an old bishop from Yugoslavia, spoke asking that the name of St. Joseph should be included in the canon of the Mass. He was difficult to understand and repetitive in his speech. The Cardinal presiding interjected with heavy irony. 'Complete your holy and eloquent speech. We all love St. Joseph and we hope there are many saints in Yugoslavia.' At the end of the session, perhaps buoyed up by the success of his intervention, the Cardinal President shouted 'St. Joseph, pray for us!' which the bishops thought a great joke. The Holy Father had been watching on closed circuit television and he knew, as the Council members, to give them their due, did not, that the bishop in question had been tortured and sentenced to four years in a concentration camp, after a long trial by the communist government. An assassination attempt had broken both his hips, his health was ruined and caused his difficulties in communication. Three days later, without reference to the Council, the Holy Father ordered that St. Joseph's name be included in the canon of the Mass.

The 'schemes' prepared by the Curia to present to the Council for consideration were not to the liking of the bishops, all of whom knew the difficulties they faced in presenting Catholic teaching in their various countries - each one presenting its own problems. Revelation, discussed in the first session was a case in point. Ultimately, Pope John himself decided to set up a special commission, including the recently established Secretariat for Promoting Christian Unity, to rework the project on the sources of revelation, thus rejecting the earlier scheme. This opened up the subject matter of the Council and allowed a clearer focus.

It became obvious that the Council would have to go into another session and it was agreed that it should reconvene on September 8th, the feast of Our Lady's Birthday. In the meantime, the bishops were to study and to keep in touch. The Holy Father's health was declining rapidly and he must have been aware that he was unlikely to be there when the Council re-assembled. So far, the bishops had considered matters pertaining to the Church herself. He was anxious that the message to the world would be proclaimed. He was to convey it himself in his encyclical, *Pacem in Terris*.

Contacts with the Soviet Union

The thawing of relations between the Holy See and Soviet Russia, however tentative and hedged round, produced one tangible good. Khruschev sent a Christmas message of greeting to the Holy Father, to which Pope John replied with 'cordial thanks... we return them from the heart in words that come from on high: Peace on earth to men of goodwill.' He enclosed two speeches on the subject of peace with justice, sealed with a picture of Our Lady and a prayer to her. At the request of the Pope, made through circumspect routes, Khrushev located the labour camp which had held Archbishop Slipyi of Ukraine, for seventeen years. In February 1963, Archbishop Slipyi was released from prison and taken to Moscow and was met by Mgr. Willebrands who told him he was free. The Archbishop's elation was punctured by the further news that he would not be allowed to go to the Ukraine. It was Rome or back to the labour camp. Very unwillingly, the Archbishop agreed to go to Rome. Had he refused, Pope John's work for accommodation with the Russians would have been in ruins at the rebuff.

In Rome, he met the Holy Father, who stretched out his arms to him, but Archbishop Slipyi knelt and kissed his feet. The Pope raised him and embraced him. They went to the Pope's chapel and said the *Magnificat* .

In Lent, Pope John made visits to parishes, and again received a heartfelt, joyous welcome. Early in March, the Pope was nominated for the Balzan Peace Prize, an award given by an international committee, four of whom were Russians, all of whom had put forward the name of Pope John. Receiving the nomination in the Vatican, the Holy Father said that he saw the award as an acknowledgement of the Church's constant work for peace, from Leo XIII to Pius XII. The Italian communist press took the opportunity to imply that the Pope supported the Soviet government and that of the satellite states. It may be that Kruschev hoped that he did! Khrushchev's son-in-law, Alexis Adjoubei, a journalist, was present with his wife at the announcement of the prize winner and requested an audience with the Holy Father. He received them as people who had courteously asked to see him and were bringing a gift from Khruschev. Pope John spoke French

to them since Khruschev's daughter spoke the language
and he gave her a rosary, saying it reminded him of his
mother, gave stamps for their three boys and sent them a
kiss, especially the youngest, Ivan, he said, because Ivan
is the Russian form of John, a name that meant so much
to him. Khruschev's daughter had tears in her eyes.
Adjoubei received coins of the Holy See and was asked
to pass on to Khruschev a medal designed by Giacomo
Manzu. He said to them 'You say you are atheists. Surely
you will receive the blessing of an old man for your
children. He blessed them as they stood with bowed
heads. 'That was only a little blessing; such a little one
can't hurt. Receive it as it was intended...in a spirit of
reconciliation. May peace and justice be with you
always.' Adjoubei asked if he could publish something
about the visit, but Pope John said 'no'.

Pacem in Terris

Shortly after this incident, the Holy Father sent his last
encyclical, *Pacem in Terris* to be published.

In the Council, the debate on the Liturgy was to be
followed by Revelation. Important as these subjects were
and, in the case of the Liturgy, far-reaching with
unexpected consequences, Pope John wanted the Council
to look at the well-being of all people of good-will in the
world, outside the walls of the Church as well as inside.
He set down his most heartfelt concerns in his new

encyclical, while he waited for the Council to catch up. It contained what he wanted to say to mankind.

In *Pacem in Terris*, Pope John considers justice and peace, freedom and order. He goes beyond *Mater et Magistra* which reads almost like a personal memoir of his family's economic strengths and weaknesses, as he considers how Europe, in particular, should build societies which reflect the common good.

Pacem in Terris, sets out his more fundamental concerns, grounding the principle of freedom in mutual trust between peoples, with 'sincerity in negotiations and faithful fulfilment of obligations, since. . .all should help to develop in others an increasing awareness of their duties, an adventurous and enterprising spirit and the resolution to take the initiative for their own advancement ....' He welcomes the help that rich countries were giving to poor countries, but he warns against any form of cultural domination.

He argues that after the use of nuclear weapons in the war against Japan, men were coming to see that mass, mutual destruction could never be tolerated. He upholds a 'public authority, with a world-wide sphere of activity', acting with the consent of the nations in order to secure the rights of the individual person, through the principle of 'subsidiarity'. Pope John takes the United Nations' 'Universal Declaration of Human Rights' as a 'goal to be sought by all nations'.

He exhorts 'Our sons ... in the light of Christian principles and with love as their guide' to involve themselves 'in the work of these institutions'. He looks for integration of spiritual values 'with those of science, technology and the professions' and blames inadequate Christian education for a disparity between faith and practice. Catholics, working with others must not compromise their faith, but they must act with understanding and unselfishness, distinguishing between 'the error' itself and the man who commits it.

Pope John is aware that in nature, everything grows slowly. There will be peace in the world only when there is peace in every human heart. This comes from accepting 'God as ruler of the mind; the mind as ruler of the body'. He impresses on his readers that, 'Our Lord, Jesus Christ, after His resurrection, stood in the midst of His disciples and said "Peace be upon you". Let us then pray with all fervour for this peace which our divine Redeemer came to bring us....' He ends with his blessing 'upon all men of goodwill ' The letter was published on Holy Thursday, April 11th, 1963. It comprises his dearest hopes and prayers.

The Pope faces death

By the time of the publication of *Pacem in Terris*, the Holy Father was suffering great pain. He had been diagnosed with stomach cancer. He courgeously attended all the services of the Holy Week Triduum. He wrote in his diary of 'A peaceful Mass at home, then abandonment to God.' He felt great joy at the reception of *Pacem in Terris* and the warmth of his reception over Easter.

The visit of Khruschev's daughter and son-in-law and the exchange of goodwill messages with the Soviet leader earlier, might have had an effect on the voters in Italy's general election on April 28th. The communists increased their vote considerably and it is possible that some people felt that they were justified in voting for them, when the Pope seemed to offer them a hand of friendship. He himself distinguished between an ideology and the people who pursued it, believing that individuals could carry out good acts, despite the faulty theories that they upheld.

Parts of the press criticised the Pope and thought that *Pacem in Terris* had pre-disposed many to vote for the communist party. Others said that the Christian Democrats had simply lost popularity. In some places, he was described as a 'naive dupe' of the communists, but he was comforted to receive a message from President Kennedy stating that the US government did not endorse those criticisms.

Despite his failing health, and terrible pain, Pope John was able to receive the Balzan Peace prize in the throne room of the Vatican on the 10th of May. He accepted it, he said, as an award to the popes of the last eighty years, all of whom had 'worked untiringly' for peace'. For

Christmas, 1963, his Secretary, Mgr, Capovilla had given him a Russian Grammar. He wrote in his diary the next night that 'I got out of bed and then kneeling before the crucified Lord, I consecrated my life and the final sacrifice of my whole being for my part in this great undertaking, the conversion of Russia to the Catholic Church'. It was part of his universal apostolate.

On May 17th, he celebrated Mass for the last time. He longed to be able to say Mass thereafter, but could only receive Holy Communion. The friar who was his night nurse said to him, 'this bed is your altar.' He replied 'You are right ... an altar needs a victim and I'm ready.'

Before he was Pope, in 1959, he wrote 'This is the mystery of my life. Do not look for other explanations... "The will of God is our peace"... The same thought it contained is in that other expression which is dear and familiar to me: "obedience and peace". I repeated it in the same spirit at Holy Mass. At noon ... I put great fervour of heart and lips into the words, "domine, tu scis quia amo te", "Lord, you know that I love you".'

In his last retreat, before the Council, he wrote a summary of 'the great graces, bestowed on a man who has a low esteem of himself:

'First Grace: To have accepted with simplicity the honour and the burden of my ponificate, with the joy of being able to say that I did nothing to obtain it, absolutely nothing... May the Lord give us strength to bring everything to a successful conclusion!...

'Second Grace: To have been able to accept as simple and capable of being immediately put into effect certain ideas which were not in the least complex in themselves...but far-reaching in their effects and full of responsibilities for the future...'

As Pope, he had also written, 'I feel I no longer have any special ties in this life, no family, no earthly country or nation...I see myself only as the humble and unworthy "servant of the servants of God". The whole world is my family... This vision, this feeling of belonging to the whole world will give a new impulse to my constant and continual daily prayer...'

When he was told that no further treatment for the cancer was possible, he simply said to his secretary and friend, 'Help me to die as a bishop or a pope should.' Just before receiving the Sacrament of the Sick, he spoke of the crucifix opposite his bed. 'Those open arms have been the programme of my pontificate: they say Christ died for all, for all. No one is excluded from his love, from his forgiveness....'

The life of Blessed Pope John XXIII, beatified by Pope John Paul II, was entirely self-consistent. His love of God as Creator, Saviour and Holy Spirit, his love of his saints, and of people in every aspect of their lives, Christian and non-Christian alike, was the theme of his eighty years. He also loved the world for all its imperfections. 'Blessed be the Pope, who has made us enjoy the world', wrote Cardinal Montini, later Pope Paul VI. He sought to make the Church immediate and loveable so that her truth could not be denied.

Vatican II, his Council, in its aftermath, brought much of the renewal for which he worked, and also the crisis with which the Church still labours.

On June 3rd, 1963, he died, at 7.49pm. The world mourned the loss of the universal parish priest.

Main Sources Consulted

The Journal of a Soul, Angelo Roncalli, Bl. Pope John XXIII, Geoffrey Chapman, 1965; *Mater et Magistra*, Bl. Pope John XXIII, 1961; *Pacem in Terris*, Bl. Pope John XXIII, Catholic Truth Society, 1963; *John XXIII, the Pope of the Council*, P. Hebblethwaite, Geoffrey Chapman, 1984; *John, the Transitional Pope*, Ernesto Balducci, Burns, Oats, 1965; *I Will be Called John*, Lawrence Elliott, Collins, 1974; *Pope John XXIII*, Meriol Trevor, Macmillan, 1967; *The Utopia of John XXIII*, Giancarlo Zizola, Orbis Books, New York, 1974; *Letters from Vatican City*, Xavier Rynne, Faber & Faber, 1963; *Vatican II, Forty Personal Stories*, W. Madges and M. Daley, 23rd Publications, Mystic, USA, 2003; *Vatican II*, Alan Schreck, Servant Books, Cincinatti, 2003